Strength For Tod.
me to tears, and
vice. Having sor
all seem to seek .... These devotions can help a mother like me who has a 40-year old son who races cars and school buses. He is in danger just as a service man is. I don't think any mother with boys is ever immune to the thoughts that their son is safe in this world. Thank you for reaching out to those mothers and even one like me. I love it.

-Bev Houseman,

(Author of *Rusty And Me, A Mother's Story,* contributor to *Chicken Soup For The Nurse's Soul, Caregiver's Soul, Grandma's Soul, Kendall Bell's Books 1&2, From The Heart; Stories of Love and Friendship,* and *Family Doctor; The Magazine That Makes House Calls,* and many other publications.)

Carol Channer's devotional book is much more than a comfort to my soul! I can't wait to read more of it each day. Up until now I wondered if I was a normal human being, feeling and thinking the thoughts each day that come into my heart and mind. She has managed to put into words what has been going through my mind!

-Donna Space, (mother of a Marine)
Corryton, Tennessee

In this book, comfort comes from many sources. The scriptures are just perfect. I believe they will resonate in the reader's soul with God's truth. The text is inspiring and will nourish the mind. When they read these words, the biggest source of comfort will come from knowing they are not alone with their thoughts and fears...Knowledge can come from reading or being told something; however, wisdom comes from persevering through difficult times and situations.

-Kathy Green (I.T. Specialist, Tupperware Brands Corp.)
Kissimmee, Florida

I just finished reading Carol Channer's devotional, *Strength For Today While My Soldier Is Away.* I found it to be uplifting, inspiring, and insightful, while being down-to-earth and enjoyable reading. It would be a perfect gift to give to any family member of a soldier. In fact, as soon as it is published, I intend to purchase some copies to keep on hand for that purpose. Carol's thoughts are so typical of what every soldier's family feels and thinks, and it helps to know that others are just like you. The spiritual guidance she offers is straight forward and simple to understand. I think that anyone would benefit from the suggestions she offers. Her book fills a gap in the available literature for the family members of soldiers.

-Gail Pankey, (mother of a Coast Guardsman)

Strength
for today while my
Soldier
is away

★

Carol J. Channer

Strength

for today while my

Soldier

is away

Tate Publishing & Enterprises

Strength For Today While My Soldier Is Away
Copyright © 2007 by Carol J. Channer. All rights reserved.

Published by Tate Publishing & Enterprises, LLC
127 E. Trade Center Terrace | Mustang, Oklahoma 73064 USA
1.888.361.9473 | www.tatepublishing.com

Tate Publishing is committed to excellence in the publishing industry. The company reflects the philosophy established by the founders, based on Psalm 68:11,
"The Lord gave the word and great was the company of those who published it."

Book design copyright © 2007 by Tate Publishing, LLC. All rights reserved.
Cover design by Isaiah McKee
Interior design by Jacob Crissup

Published in the United States of America

ISBN: 978-1-60247-813-8
1. Christian/Inspirational   2. Soldier at War (for family)
07.10.11

Psalm 91 (NKJV)
"The Soldier's Prayer"
Safety of Abiding in the Presence of God

He who dwells in the secret place of the Most High
Shall abide under the shadow of the Almighty.
I will say of the Lord, "He is my refuge and my fortress;
My God, in Him I will trust."
Surely He shall deliver you from the snare of the fowler
And from the perilous pestilence.
He shall cover you with His feathers,
And under His wings you shall take refuge;
His truth shall be your shield and buckler.
You shall not be afraid of the terror by night,
Nor of the arrow that flies by day,
Nor of the pestilence that walks in darkness,
Nor of the destruction that lays waste at noonday.

A thousand may fall at your side,
And ten thousand at your right hand;
But it shall not come near you.
Only with your eyes shall you look,
And see the reward of the wicked.

Because you have made the Lord, who is my refuge,
Even the Most High, your dwelling place,
No evil shall befall you,
Nor shall any plague come near your dwelling;
For He shall give His angels charge over you,
To keep you in all your ways.
In their hands they shall bear you up,
Lest you dash your foot against a stone.
You shall tread upon the lion and the cobra,
The young lion and the serpent you shall trample
underfoot.

"Because he has set his love upon Me, therefore I will
deliver him;
I will set him on high, because he has known My name.
He shall call upon Me, and I will answer him;

I will be with him in trouble;
I will deliver him and honor him.
With long life I will satisfy him,
And show him My salvation."

Acknowledgements

Strength For Today While My Soldier Is Away is inspired by and dedicated to my son, Specialist James Joseph Channer, U.S. Army. Thank you, Joe, for being the most wonderful son in the world!

I also wish to honor my other family members who are currently serving our nation in the military: son-in-love SPC David K. Ramey, U.S. Army; nephew Jonathan B. Pankey, U.S. Coast Guard; cousin Jack Helmer, U.S. Army, cousin Jack Bartlett, U.S. Air Force Reserves; and his son, John, also in the U.S.A.F.R. I love you all and my prayers go out daily for each of you.

Wayne, you are my wonderful, hard-working

husband and the forever love of my life. Jennifer, Kimberly, and my new daughter-in-love, Nicole: my beautiful, strong, independent daughters, you each make my heart sing with joy! Mikah Mae, precious granddaughter, you make every day special!

Special thanks to both Beverly Houseman and Lynne Johnson, who proofread my work, and shared invaluable insight and information. Thank you for your encouragement all along the way.

I wish to mention several other deserving young friends who have made the unselfish decision to serve during this time of war. Their loved ones waiting here at home have motivated me to finish this project. Nathan S., Kyle E., Brandon W., Matt B., Daniel K., Mike S., Joe M., and so many others. We are so very proud of you! Stay safe.

I ask God's richest blessings to be upon each reader who is missing his or her favorite soldier, and I pray that the Lord will cover every one of our soldiers with His constant protection.

To the families who have suffered the ultimate sacrifice during this war, I will steadfastly trust God

to sustain you and comfort your hearts. Our deepest sympathies go out to you with love and prayers.
We, your fellow countrymen, are indebted to you.
You and your soldier will forever be cherished in
our hearts.

-Carol Channer

Contents

Preface

Your soldier. Perhaps your son or daughter, your husband or wife. Maybe your soldier is your mother, father, brother, sister, or some other relative or close friend...my soldier is my son.

James Joseph was only eighteen years old, fresh out of high school, when he left for basic training. He is doing what he believes he was born to do: serve his country in the United States Army.

Yes, we are proud of him, so very proud! But, we are a country at war, and so, we are also frightened to the very core of our souls. If your soldier is away, you know this fear well.

Whoever your soldier is, wherever he or she is

stationed in this world, you need God's strength being renewed daily in your life to be able to get through each day.

Some days are good days; filled with great faith, peace and patience, yet many other days are worrisome; splattered with doubts and fears, shy on faith and trust.

This little book is written with a prayer that it will lessen the dark moments and keep our waiting eyes focused upon our awesome God who dearly loves us, and loves our soldiers.

Especially on those days when your heart is heavy, remember the words of the psalmist: *"Be still, and know that I am God"* (Psalm 46:10 NIV). Once again make a deliberate choice to place your heart, and your soldier, in His Hands.

God will give you the strength you need to go about your day and not just muddle through! No! God will make it a good day full of faith, peace, and yes, even joy! His own dear Presence will be at your side, lending aid and comfort, moment by moment by moment. May God bless you as you read this, and may God bless and protect your precious soldier.

Introduction

While her only son prepared to join the Army, Carol Channer began to scour stores for a book on the subject of sending a child off to war. Finding none, she began journaling her own feelings, fears, and frustrations, as the Lord began to plant an idea within her spirit to pen a devotional book aimed directly at the heart of our military families.

Strength For Today While My Soldier Is Away is a compilation of thoughts, reflections, poetry, Scripture, and prayers intended to move the reader away from worry and fear; redirecting their attention to the wonderful provisional grace of the Lord.

Invoking both tears and laughter, this devotional book is written in a manner that allows the reader to quickly peruse a few pages at a time. It is enjoyable when being read from beginning to end, or simply opened to a random page.

Everyone who loves a soldier will enjoy reading *Strength For Today While My Soldier Is Away.*

Written with heartfelt prayers that our military family members will find support and comfort within its pages, the author hopes that each reader will be encouraged to seek for themselves a deep and enriching daily relationship with the Lord.

Peace

How shall we find peace
During this time of war?
Carry on with our lives
Fearing what lies in store?
Where can we find mercy?
What help should we seek?
Dust off your old Bible
Take more than a peek!
The key to life's troubles,
The peace that we need,
Will leap from the pages -
If only we'll read!
Do you see Jesus loves you?

Feel the Spirit's soft tug?
Within the pages you'll feel
Our Father's warm hug!
Seeking refuge 'mid turmoil,
As our prayers to God rise;
In His Holy Word find
The power to change lives.

Seeing God

"Then their eyes were opened, and they recognized him".

Luke 24:31*a* NIV

Walking through the woods early one morning, I was earnestly searching for deer. I was hoping to catch a glimpse of what I consider to be one of God's most glorious creatures, but this day, though I was looking, I was simply not seeing. My eyes scanned the forest, but saw no deer.

Suddenly it occurred to me that we sometimes look for God in this same manner; seeking, scanning, even perhaps looking right smack at Him, and yet, still missing Him completely. I wondered if this happens because we have not spent enough time training our eyes to see Him properly.

Maybe if I came to the woods early every morning, I would be better at spotting the deer I knew had to be there! We must focus our eyes, as well as our hearts and minds, to see God as He wants, not as we expect Him to be.

Just as that thought finished forming in my mind, there she was; a large, lovely doe, standing still, very near, watching me intently. God, too, is right there with us, ever-present, watching, waiting patiently for our eyes to fix upon Him. Sometimes we need to simply be still and focus.

Lord, help me to stand still, even if only for a few moments today. Long enough to calm my thoughts and fix them, and my eyes, upon Your glorious face. Allow me to see what it is that You want me to understand about Yourself today. Whatever my soldier faces this day, allow him to see You, to feel Your presence, Your power, and Your protection, so that he can know how much he is loved, by both of us!

The Weekend Before Basic

I peered out the window at my family playing in the rain like children. *Crazy goofs,* I'm thinking smugly from safe inside my car, away from the wind, rain and lightning...and, *What's this?*

Laughter?

Those goofs were having a great time together out there in the middle of a sudden summer thunderstorm! I pulled out my camera and took a few snapshots, not even thinking that this was the last few moments of actual family life, before our soldier was to leave home.

My family was safe together, happy together, dancing and playing in the rain. Mischievously, they yelled at the sky: *Go ahead, storm, do your best!*

Suddenly it occurred to me that in just a few days, we'd no longer be together; perhaps we would never dance in the rain as a family again. With tears in my eyes, I leapt from the car and joined in the dance.

Let those thunderclouds roll in. We're a family, and together we are invincible! No amount of distance between us can ever change that! This is one of those precious moments that I'll treasure forever and ever.

> *"But let all who take refuge in you be glad; let them ever sing for joy. Spread your protection over them, that those who love your name may rejoice in you. For surely, O* LORD, *you bless the righteous; you surround them with your favor as with a shield"*.

Psalm 5:11–12 NIV

Godly Reminders

"Look to the LORD *and his strength; seek his face always"*

1 Chronicles 16:11 NIV

Ever since my soldier left home, I've found that I must be more diligent than ever about spending time with God. It's too easy to neglect God in the hectic rush of daily activities.

One thing that helps me is to take a few minutes many times during the day to reflect on and hold conversations with God. It might be helpful to keep several reminders around, such as a devotional calendar by the kitchen sink, a daily Bible verse posted in the bathroom, or as a screensaver on the computer. Keep several Bibles handy; one lying open on the sofa, another at the night stand, and a small devotional booklet tucked inside your purse. This method allows you to have moments with God right at your fingertips all throughout the day.

Reminders of my soldier are everywhere, so it really helps me to keep reminders of my Savior all around, too!

Heavenly Father, thank You for the small tokens that remind me of my soldier, but, Lord, I especially want to say thank You for all the beauty that surrounds me that keeps my mind focused on You, for it is truly Your presence in my life that means the world to me.

God's Calming Voice

"He replied, 'You of little faith, why are you so afraid?' Then he got up and rebuked the winds and the waves, and it was completely calm".

Matthew 8:26 NIV

God still speaks to us in a small, quiet voice. We can understand Him only if we are paying close attention. God also still calms the storms whenever He wishes.

If you have prayed for the storms in your life to cease, yet they continue to rage on, perhaps God is actually speaking to you in His still, small voice; saying, *"Be still. Know that I am God. Peace, be still."*

Sometimes we are so busy fighting the storm, we forget that all we really need to do is reach for our Father's hand.

Sometimes the storms of life are hurricanes; steady, fierce rains and winds pounding at you from all sides. Other times it may be a tornado, fast and devastating. Sometimes they are more like enormous waves that seem to knock you down when you are not expecting it. Sometimes waves of fear and worry over your soldier will seemingly come out of nowhere and catch you off guard.

No matter what kind of storm, you are not equipped to handle it on your own, but God can easily handle any storm!

Remember, too, that when you've fought the storm with all of your strength until you have none left, that God is patiently waiting by your side for you to turn your problems over to Him. He has plenty of strength that you can use! When you have none, He has plenty.

If you're feeling overwhelmed, take a break. Go for a walk, or simply sit down and be quiet, wait, and listen for God's whisper, *"You are my child and I AM still in control! Peace, My child; be still!"* The stormy winds may continue to howl, but you will discover that God has once again given you the strength you need for this moment, and for this day. You, like the disciples of Jesus, may even find yourself overwhelmed at His capacity to bring about such wonderful serenity.

> *"The men were amazed and asked, 'What kind of man is this? Even the winds and the waves obey him'".*
>
> Matthew 8:27 NIV

First Phone Call

Do you remember receiving that first, long-awaited phone call from your soldier? How wonderful to hear that special voice!

At the end of our first, much-too-short conversation with our soldier, I suddenly burst into unexpected tears! Tears of happiness and sadness mingled together into one sobbing mass! Tears of relief, thanking the Lord that my soldier was well. Tears of loneliness from missing him so very much. Tears of joy at just being able to actually speak with him. Tears of sorrow and heartache for all those kindred spirits who will never again receive such a call from their soldier.

I asked God to encourage the hearts of all of those whose soldiers are not allowed to make calls home because of security or locale, and for those that are not even permitted to know where their soldier is stationed. I realized that my own soldier could be included in that group much too soon.

I mentally reviewed every word of our brief talk; trying to memorize the inflection of his voice, the excitement of the moment, and attempting to draw in all the depth of feelings I was experiencing.

After some time of tears and prayer, I rose; energized by the awareness that this wonderful phone call had given me all the strength that I'll need for today and maybe tomorrow, too!

Thank You, dear Lord, for the wonderful gift of a conversation with my loved one. Precious moments as simple as this remind us that You care about every aspect of our lives. Please keep my soldier safe until our next phone call!

Reflections Of Jesus
(A Poem for the New Year)

Does He show in my face…?
Do I let His Light shine…?
Can you see Him in my walk…?
Is His reflection in mine?
As I start a new year
With its hopes and its schemes
Did I remember to place Him
Ahead of my dreams?
If we meet one another,
I pray that you'll see
Reflections of Jesus
Abiding in me.

Cuddles

"And my God will meet all your needs according to his glorious riches in Christ Jesus".

Philippians 4:19 NIV

Pets. Oh, how we love and spoil our precious pets, don't we? One of our family's menagerie is Cuddles, a tiny dark calico cat who has determined that her life's work is to be at the side of her human masters as much of the time as she possibly can.

Cuddles is most content when one of her humans is sitting on a bed, where she can curl up beside them and purr. If a hand should stretch toward her, that's even better! But, if her human rises to leave,

Cuddles immediately springs into action, trying everything within her power to convince them to stay right there with her. It has apparently never occurred to her that her five-pound body and tiny paws cannot stop a large human from moving past her. Nor has the fact that she doesn't succeed ever stop her from trying again the next time. Besides, often enough, her feeble attempts to hold on to her master will result in a final scratch on the head or a rub down her back, so, to Cuddles, the reward is well worth her effort.

I think God wants me to be more like Cuddles; content to sit in His presence, gaze lovingly into His face, with quiet praise songs purring from my heart, and a deep reluctance to ever lose sight of Him for even a moment.

Cuddles knows that her happiness is simply being with her master. Our lives will also be filled with joy and contentment when we remain in the presence of our Lord, who loves us completely and supplies all of our needs.

Lord God Almighty, allow me to remain in Your presence today. I simply want to gaze at Your beauty and sing praises to Your name. I miss my soldier so very much today, Lord, but by being with You, I know I can be content. My loving Master can take care of my aching heart as well as supply everything my soldier needs. I will choose to sit beside You and be comforted by our closeness today.

Inner Peace

As I withdraw into the quiet peacefulness of the woods, I am in awe of God's creative touch in everything I see around me. Yet, I am perplexed. How is it that God's greatest creation of all, mankind, has strayed so far from His perfect plan?

My heart asks, "Why war, Lord?" I wonder why every man cannot simply stop, see God's hand controlling everything in nature, and realize the futility in fighting among themselves. *If we could all just surrender to You, Lord God, then all of our soldiers everywhere could come home safely!*

But, there will not be peace in the world, I know. All I can do today is trust God to take care of my needs, protect my soldier, and, then, of course, I must try not to get angry at that crazy driver who will cut me off in traffic later today!

I must simply ask the Lord to help me be a peaceful person today. I need to let Him fill me with an inner peace that will radiate to those around me.

I have to choose to remember the quiet beauty I have seen this morning in the creations of God's woods, and the peacefulness that permeates everything in the forest.

I must strive to become just as calm and serene within my own soul. I can trust that God's peace, thriving within me, gives me all the strength I need for today.

> *Dear Creator Father, I truly want to see You in everything around me today; in the smallest flower, or the breeze in my hair. Please help me decide this day to be at peace; with myself, with others, and with Your Perfect Plan. Allow my soldier a way to have this same blessing. And, Lord, in the same caring manner that You protect even the small-*

est of Your creatures with camouflage, please also cover my soldier, and all of our soldiers, with Your protection and bring them safely through the day and the night. Allow them to feel our love while You guide and direct their every step.

"How Are You Doing?"

"How are you doing?" This phrase was once simply a pleasant greeting, not really needing or expecting a genuine answer. But now, people who know us, and know that our soldier is away, ask this same question, usually with a touch on the arm or eye-to-eye contact. I realize they are asking from their hearts, so I try not to just brush it off with a "fine, fine" anymore. Now I am so incredibly moved by their true concern that I cannot give a pat answer. The intent behind the question deserves an honest reply. I highly value their friendship and prayers, so my response must reflect my gratitude.

Sometimes I suddenly find myself fighting back

tears at this question. This is a new sensation that I am still learning to deal with! Lately, though, I can usually smile and manage to say something truthful.

Out of gratitude toward God for all the strength He has given me day-by-day, I frequently try to mention the importance of staying focused on the Lord, instead of my soldier. This sometimes will open a door to a deeper spiritual conversation. Wow! It always feels so fantastic when God works like that!

I know that if my soldier being away helps bring someone else into a closer relationship with God, then our sacrifice is worthwhile. That reminds me of the enormous sacrifice our Heavenly Father made for us; allowing His only Son to bear the penalty for all our sins by death upon a cross.

Considering this renews my faith, and *Ah-Ha!* A friendly question, "How are you doing?" So simple, and yet I suddenly discover that, once again, I have all the strength I need for today!

Thank You, Lord, for giving us friends who truly care about us!

Soothing Music

"My heart is steadfast, O God; I will sing and make music with all my soul".

Psalm 108:1 NIV

Dealing with loneliness is one of the many difficult issues we now face on a daily basis. It sometimes seems to permeate every inch of our homes and our lives. Shortly after my soldier left home, my husband also had to be away most of the time due to his job requirements. It was a difficult time for us.

Filling your empty home with your favorite music can be helpful sometimes. Turn on a CD or radio instead of the TV set. That old cliché about music soothing the mortal soul holds a great deal of truth!

On those days when my heart is aching from missing my soldier, I allow music to sooth and strengthen me. Sometimes, it's upbeat, old rock classics from my youth that make me move. I clean, paint, or write, and time passes quickly.

Some days I listen to my soldier's favorite CDs, to make it seem like he's still right there in his room. I crank them up and close the door, just like he did!

Other days I enjoy old hymns or praise music, which redirects my focus away from the emptiness around me towards the fullness and goodness of the Lord. God often uses the words of the music to gently speak to my heart.

"Do not grieve, for the joy of the Lord is your strength".

Nehemiah 8:10 NIV

Answered Prayer

A friend sent an email request for prayer over an urgent need, and within hours, people from all over the world were praying; even people unknown to the family! It was wonderful to get the report shortly after that God had answered this request and the need was met. It is good to know that we still have "prayer warriors" to whom we can turn in time of need. It is also comforting to know that God not only hears and answers our prayers, but also is merciful and gracious enough toward us to allow us to see the reality of answered prayer in our lives.

This strengthens our faith and encourages us to continue to take our requests to our Heavenly

Father. Whenever our faith wavers, we can look back and remember the many times when our Father met our needs in the past, which helps us to trust that He is quite able to handle our needs today, as well.

God encourages believers to come boldly before His throne with our requests. As a good daddy wants to give his children everything they need, so our Lord truly delights in meeting our needs daily. We can place our soldiers into His care and trust that He will be with them no matter what they face today.

> *"Let us therefore come boldly to the throne of grace, that we may obtain mercy and find grace to help in time of need".*
>
> Hebrews 4:16 KJV

The Fully Broken Promise of God

There's never been a Promise
That God has forsaken,
No Promise in which our Lord was mistaken,
No Promise made that His Hand hath not kept,
Nor one over which His tears have not wept-

When we, His people,
Become crushed and broken;
Hearts full of sorrow, repentant words spoken;
Then we have become the Promise of God,
Beloved, empowered, feet fully shod-
Doing His work here on earth as we stay
Fulfilling His plan for our life while we may

Forever protected wherever we trod…
The fully broken Promise of God!

Living for Jesus each step of the way,
Dependant on Him each moment, each day.
Kept by His hand, fed by His Word,
Knowing His voice sweetest ere to be heard,

Trusting that we will ne'er be forsaken,
Knowing that He is never mistaken.
Assured we are kept by His Infinite Hand,
His tears for us fallen unmeasured as sand,

Knowing He smiles and gives us a nod
When we are a fully broken Promise of God

Some Days Drag On

"When I called, you answered me; you made me bold and stouthearted".

Psalm 138:3 NIV

I sometimes ask God why it seems that certain days fly by quickly and easily while other days seem to drag on forever. I'd like to have my focus so fixed upon the Lord that all my days flow swiftly and serenely along! Yet, I am so easily distracted, and as soon as I am looking at anything other than the Savior, my day goes off-kilter.

Since my soldier went away, I've become aware of this more than ever before. Now, as soon as I realize that my day is dragging along, I try to quickly stop and do something to bring my mind into God's presence. I turn away from life's storm and take refuge in the Lord.

To accomplish this, I sometimes just take a moment to gaze at the sky, look at the birds, the clouds, or whatever nature happens to be around me. Other times I turn to the pages of my Bible, or sing a hymn, or just begin to thank God for the blessings in my life and praise Him for being everything I need. I then say a prayer for my soldier and all of our soldiers away, and for their loved ones.

Amazingly, such a simple action brings a wonderful sense of order to even the most unbearable days. God honors us by giving His grace, peace, and strength when we honor Him through our actions, thoughts, prayers and praises.

By taking a few moments to reflect on God and glorify Him, He will reward you with whatever amount of strength you need; probably more than enough to go through your day today.

Doing Daily Chores

"Whatever your hand finds to do, do it with all your might".

Ecclesiastes 9:10 NIV

Mundane chores are something I used to hate doing: laundry, dishes, lawn mowing, sweeping, gardening...you know, those thankless jobs that need to be done again just as soon as you've finished them!

While your soldier is away, however, these routine chores begin to take a new form. They can be a blessing! Sometimes, you can throw yourself into them, allowing your mind to rest from troublesome thoughts and focus on the task at hand.

Other times, you can do them by rote, letting your mind wander, and even thinking about your soldier who may also be performing some routine task at that very same moment!

When the job is done, don't move quickly on to the next task. Take a moment to sit back and admire your accomplishment: the beautiful lawn, the clean bathtub, the pile of bills paid. *Ahh…*

Now allow yourself just a minute to be satisfied! This can renew your spirit in a special way that you may not even realize.

God will bless those busy hands, and when you survey the finished job, you will be satisfied with yourself, with God, and even with life itself!

The Lord often uses "mindless work" as a time for renewal. He will replenish your strength so that you can keep on going. You'll find that He has blessed you with the strength you need to finish the monotonous chores that await you today. At the end of the day, you can be abundantly content with your achievements!

Reaching Out for Help

The house is empty and much too quiet. Sometimes the loneliness is overwhelming. Even in the midst of a crowd, shopping, at a party, or in church, I can feel very solitary. Loneliness strikes!

Most of the time being by myself is not a bother for me. I can fill the time in many ways. However, on certain days it seems to envelop me like a big, hollow echo. I feel like it will smother me. On those days, I need help. I've learned that I cannot just sit there and wait for a friend to drop by or the phone to ring. I have to make the first move. Reaching out for help is difficult when you've been a strong person for most of your life, but I'm learning how important it is to show a little weakness every now and then. In our weakness, God gives strength.

When your life seems to reverberate with empty loneliness, don't be afraid to reach out. Call a friend. Even better, call another person who is also missing his or her soldier. You may just make their day, and your own aching void will be eased.

Sometimes I find that, even though it seemed to take all of my being to just reach for that telephone, after I've done it, I miraculously have all the strength I need to continue with my daily chores, or the peace of mind to allow me to sleep through the night.

> *"Let each of you look out not only for his own interests, but also for the interests of others"*.
>
> Philippians 2:4 NKJV

Worry

"He replied, 'If you have faith as small as a mustard seed, you can say to this mulberry tree, "Be uprooted and planted in the sea,"' and it will obey you"

Luke 17:6 NIV

Worry. It's that nagging little thing that creeps into our thoughts and robs us of our joy, our peace, our sleep.

Our Lord tells us not to worry, to remember that He is in control, that as He takes care of the least of His creations, all the more He will take care of us, His Masterpiece!

Still…sometimes worry just has a way of sneaking in and taking over. We must not give it a foothold. We must drive it out of our minds much like we would chase a critter from our porch with a broom!

We must make a concerted effort to turn our mind away from worry and quickly focus on God and His goodness. He has a plan for our lives; a perfect plan, and all we need to do is surrender to Him.

It only takes a wee bit of faith. Even on our darkest days, we can muster a wee bit, can't we?

Dear Father God, help me muster up just a wee bit more faith today; enough to say out loud, "I trust You, Lord!" Help me, then, to relax and give You control over the situation. Help me sweep out every tiny speck of worry from my mind. Be with my soldier today, Lord. Grant both of us peace of mind and help us to trust You completely.

Our Boots

There's an old saying about walking a mile in some-one else's shoes, but, as military family members, I believe we all trudge around in big, old, heavy *boots,* not shoes!

God knows what it's like to have a child leave the shelter of home, go off to war, and even to make the ultimate sacrifice. God's Son Jesus did just that!

Our God is a Father who has walked in these boots, so He can give comfort as no one else ever could. Therefore, today, I will rest in God's arms, cry with my face buried into His chest, and fall into peaceful rest, safe in His arms.

Today I will believe that my soldier is safe in God's care, perfectly protected by His angels, guided constantly by His hand. My soldier is serving his God as well as his country. I know that he is well equipped for duty and that he's got his boots on, too!

> *"Though an army besiege me, my heart will not fear; though war break out against me, even then will I be confident"*.

Psalm 27:3 NIV

Coping with the News

"Be strong and of good courage, do not fear nor be afraid of them; for the LORD your God, He is the One who goes with you. He will not leave you nor forsake you".

Deuteronomy 31:6 NKJV

Some days, I simply cannot bring myself to watch the television news for even one more minute!

If I allow it to catch me off guard, anger takes over. Suddenly, I'm overwhelmed by it all. My soldier is away, our world is in deep turmoil, and these insane terrorists are trying to destroy everything we love!

I have to fight off anger almost daily. To do this, I remind myself again that *God* is in control here, even amidst all of this awful mess, and His goodness will prevail.

When the news from far away is overwhelming, *stop!* Turn off the old news, and pick up the Good News. Yes, turn to the Bible instead of the TV set! Allow God to replace your anger with His peace, and your fears with His knowledge. You may not have enough of these to get through today, but God surely has more than enough for all of us.

Lord, please help us to seek Your face today. Replace our weaknesses with Your strengths. Stay with our soldiers and bring them safely home to us as quickly as possible!

Memories

Wasn't it only yesterday that we sat on the floor together playing with GI Joe™ toys?

In our house, these little men were never put away. They played with Pooh™ and his friends, the Transformers™ gang, all sorts of dinosaurs, Hot Wheels™, ninjas, and a whole host of other toys that were all eventually outgrown. Other toys came and went, but the GI Joes™ always stood ready.

Now, even though my soldier is away, there, in his room are his "men." All his beloved Joes still stand, patiently awaiting the return of their old commander. Will he ever return?

I realize that my soldier will probably only come home for short visits from now on. I understand that he will someday have a house of his own, and hopefully his own little boy who will enjoy playing with the old Joes. But I, like the Joes, still earnestly await his return home, every single day.

Lord, help me remember to watch as anxiously for Your return as I do my soldier's return! Remind me whenever I look at the clouds or the moon or the sunrise that, at any moment, You could return. Help me to stay focused on You, Lord, and steadfastly trust that You will keep my soldier safe again today.

Self-Pity

"You turned my wailing into dancing; you removed my sackcloth and clothed me with joy that my heart may sing to you and not be silent".

Psalm 30:11–12 NIV

Wallowing in self pity is a clear sign that I am not centering my life around Christ. Having a pity-party for myself is certainly not pleasing to Him!

The best way I have found to break this cycle of self-centeredness is to deliberately focus my attention on the needs of others. Visiting a local nursing home, calling an elderly friend, mowing the neighbor's lawn as well as my own are some great ways to fend off self pity.

There's a multitude of ways to change your own focus by focusing on others. Self pity is one of the most destructive forces we must keep out of our lives, especially while our soldiers are away.

Don't allow self pity to get you down today!

Lord, help me today to see the needs of others around me, and focus my attention on someone other than myself. When my soldier returns, let me be found busy helping others. Let me remember the examples that Jesus has given us through His servant-nature while He lived on earth among men, and both mirror and reflect His nature through my actions.

Our Hearts

"'Even now,' declares the LORD, 'return to me with all your heart, with fasting and weeping and mourning.' Rend your heart and not your garments. Return to the LORD your God, for he is gracious and compassionate, slow to anger and abounding in love, and he relents from sending calamity".

Joel 2:12–13 NIV

God looks at our hearts; not the outward trappings we use to fool other people. God wants my heart broken so that He can pour out His grace, compassion, patience, and love.

My soldier may be in my heart, but God must *have* my heart. When I offer my whole heart to God, He will treat it as a priceless treasure, and everything that is in my heart, including my soldier, is also held gently in His wonderful, gentle, loving hand.

God says in the book of Joel that He will not send calamity. That's a promise I can trust in today. Anything that happens is under God's control, and my soldier and I are both safe in His hands.

Whenever my heart feels heavy I will remember the words of this prophet and return to the LORD my God, for He is gracious and compassionate.

Lord Jesus, through the gentle prompting of the Holy Spirit, please help me to act with a pure heart today. Protect me from the evil one who tries constantly to turn my view inward and my heart black, and help me to focus on Your purity and love. If my soldier is feeling heavy-hearted today, please comfort him and allow him to feel Your presence, too.

My God Satisfies

Lord, help me to serve you with my life today,
In the palm of Your hand is where I want to stay
If the paths ahead grow rocky and steep
And the rivers to cross become murky and deep
I know that Your arms will carry me through
And as I go on I shall always praise You.

As the countless faithful who have gone on before
I shall not dread that which lies at my door
And feeling Your Presence, trusting Your grace
Lord allow me to love You, whatever I face
With all of my life, with Your grace and peace
Praise from my lips shall not ever cease

No matter what comes, Your love I'll proclaim
The songs of my soul rejoice in Your Name
You fill me with joy; wipe the tears from my eye
Put a spring in my step with Your peace from on high
Wherever I'm sent, no matter the task
I'm honored to do everything that You ask.

May Your Words fill my mouth, Your work fill my hands
My heart fills with worship as I follow Your plans
Be the day full of sunshine or bleak storms arise
I will trust Lord Jehovah, My God satisfies!
With all of my courage and strength I'll obey
Because I just want to serve You with my life today.

Finding Balance

Usually I like the busy days the most; those days when I hit the floor running and don't even look at my watch until it's late in the afternoon, and I realize that I haven't even eaten lunch yet.

Sometimes, though, I long for a quiet day; a day for working on a craft project, allowing my mind to relax, or having coffee with a friend. A day just to take a breath!

Most days I prefer to stay busy because I'm afraid if I slow down for very long I will miss my soldier too much; yet, the Lord knows that I need balance. I need to be both busy and quiet for my health and my sanity!

Overdoing can lead to exhaustion of body and mind, so be accepting of the quiet moments that God provides. These are the times that God uses to refuel your tank and give you enough strength to continue on. Balance the business with serenity.

Lord help me stay busy, but also allow me to recognize opportunities You give to rest, and help me to accept those moments as a time to unwind and refocus. Help me today to not fear the quiet times because it will be then that You will renew my strength.

Thoughtless Remarks

Sometimes people say the wrong things. Ignorant, mean, misguided, or thoughtless words that cause pain. I'd like to snap a quick one-liner back at them, but, hard as it is, I must try not to do so.

Instead, I attempt to picture my Lord Jesus being ridiculed by the people and still continuing to love and forgive them. I try to remind myself that I, too, am often guilty of saying the wrong thing and then wishing I could take back my words.

It is naturally harder to accomplish this when the irritating remarks are aimed at your soldier. It's hard to keep a civil tongue when you pass a group of so-called "peace advocates" who are hurling vicious words, and sometimes even rocks! The world is not only filled with our known terrorist enemies; we have many anti-freedom enemies that walk amongst us daily.

Jesus faced these enemies, too, and has set the example for us.

The next time someone says something hurtful about your soldier, be gentle in your response. Remember that God is your strength, and He's been there, too.

"Keep your tongue from evil and your lips from speaking lies".

Psalm 34:13 NIV

Heavenly TLC

Some days it just hits me: my soldier is away! An enormous wave of missing him washes over me. I don't even see it coming, but there I am, suddenly down with the wind knocked out of me!

These are the times when I really need a little extra tender loving care. There are many wonderful verses in the Bible that we can turn to in times like this, but one of my favorites comes from Isaiah. *"As a mother comforts her child, so will I comfort you"* (Isaiah 66:13 NIV).

Now that's a verse I can understand! Being a mother of three, a new grandmother, and a swimming instructor for many years, I know how I can comfort a child. I hold them close, talking softly, kissing them, rocking, stroking their hair, singing to them. I'm great at cuddling! Yes, that's exactly what I need from God! The same way I comfort a hurting child is the same way my heavenly Father will comfort me!

When I feel that need to be comforted, instead of moping, I try to take a few minutes to read my Bible. I curl up in bed or on the sofa with a cup of hot tea and choose favorite, old familiar passages that speak words of love and concern and my heart takes comfort. Then I add a little time spent in prayer for my soldier and praise for my King to release my tears and stress. This brings peace and consolation to my inner being, and that's the best TLC in the universe!

Be Content With God

These seem to be the darkest days;
Sometimes it's hard to see God's ways,
Our health is failing, our journey long,
We do not know where we belong.
Drugs and alcohol abound,
Planes are crashing to the ground.
Kids aren't safe within school walls;
Danger lurks throughout the halls
Ethnic cleansing, bombs and wars;
People dying by the scores
Flood and flame, earthquake, rain;
Tornado, famine, hurricane…
We cannot plan what we shall do,

Not knowing when, what, where or who-
We cannot know what plight we face,
But we can walk in love and grace
Dismay and fear will surely cease,
As we brave each day with hope and peace,
By trusting God, Who's Word is True;
We can find contentment, too.
It is the only way to live,
When all the world is churning-
It is the only hope we have to satisfy our yearning.
Be content with God each day,
Trust Him to guide you 'long the way
Read His Word, and you will see,
His promises are true-
You can live a happy life, within His Will for you!
While life is hurling, whirling past,
The Word will hold you grounded fast
To be content with God today,
Simply trust, love, and obey.

Overcoming Fear

"For God hath not given us the spirit of fear; but of power, and of love, and of a sound mind".

2 Timothy 1:7 KJV

One cannot stay in a constant state of fear. Immediately following September 11, 2001, we were all frightened. As time went on, however, we eventually began living our normal daily lives again.

The human spirit seems unable to live in perpetual fear. Perhaps that is why so many innocent Middle-Eastern people continue to be blown up by terrorist bombs on their city buses and in their marketplaces. Knowing that a suicide bomber is a very real possibility, they resolutely go about their daily routine, even though it means putting themselves in a vulnerable position.

Yes, I fear for my soldier's safety, but constantly dwelling on that would not do either of us any good. I simply must set aside fearful thoughts and once again place my trust into God's hands. Living in fear is not living for Christ. Some days, I have to repeat that to myself again and again until I get the message!

I will trust in Thee, my Lord, and I will not succumb to my worries and fears today. In whatever my soldier faces this day, grant Your courage. Help us both to remember that when we have no bravery left within us, You have plenty that You are more than willing to share.

Having Faith

My soldier has chosen an honorable profession. I am very proud of him for the maturity he has shown. His patriotism, his courage and his complete trust in God are signs of the kind of faith that America was founded upon.

My soldier trusts that God will take care of him, at the same time knowing that if he should die, he will be with the Lord, and that the Lord will carry his grieving family through the worst time imaginable.

There was once a short time span when my soldier's faith did waver. Knowing this, I prayed even harder for him, for I knew he was in so much more danger than we could ever imagine. I also know that the unhappiest people in the world are Christians who are living outside of their faith.

Watching God restore my soldier's faith was a wonderful experience that I believe strengthened my faith as much as it did my soldier's.

Now he has a mature faith in God, far beyond his years. If my soldier can trust God completely today, then so can I!

> *"God is our refuge and strength, an ever-present help in trouble".*
>
> Psalm 46:1 NIV

Praising God

"Praise the LORD. Praise, O servants of the LORD,
praise the name of the LORD. Let the name of
the LORD be praised, both now and forevermore.
From the rising of the sun to the place where it sets,
the name of the LORD is to be praised. The LORD
is exalted over all the nations, his glory above the
heavens. Who is like the LORD our God, the One
who sits enthroned on high, who stoops down to
look on the heavens and the earth?".

Psalm 113:1–6 NIV

Journaling your praises is a wonderful way to lift
your spirits. Re-reading your words in times of

doubt and fear can fill your soul with peace and comfort. Journaling your thoughts, uncertainties, prayers, and especially praises is an excellent way to grow in your faith. It allows God to fill your mind with good thoughts and keep your hands busy at the same time! You don't even need a special book or fancy pen. I encourage you to start a journal. On days when praising God seems hard to do, grab your journal and read your own words aloud to the Lord. Your plain notebook, penciled with your thoughts of prayer and praise will become a beautiful worship song to the ears of your heavenly Father.

Praise benefits me physically, mentally, and spiritually all at the same time. We are built for praise, commanded and programmed to praise our wonderful God and King. When I miss my soldier today, I'll praise God with my heart, my mind, my written words, and my voice!

> *"Then a voice came from the throne, saying: "Praise our God, all you his servants, you who fear him, both small and great!".*
>
> Revelation 19:5 NIV

Facing Change

Changes are something we face every day. Sometimes change is welcomed like a breath of fresh air, but often we resist change. It makes us uncomfortable, frightens us, or exasperates us!

As changes in many areas of my life seem to swirl me into a state of dizziness, I am glad to be able to cling to a God who does not change. I have a deeper understanding of some of the old, wonderful hymns of our faith that talk of standing on the solid Rock, leaning on Jesus, and building my hope on Christ. Many of these hymns have brought solace to my soul lately.

My soldier is facing many enormous changes,

too. I pray daily for the Lord to show Himself strong and steady in my young soldier's life. It gives me peace to know that, even amongst all the changes in our lives, we both have the constant love of the Heavenly Father who is controlling and upholding our lives.

Thank You, Lord, for being a firm foundation for my soldier and me to stand safely on, even during times of upheaval and change!

Mourning

"My soul is weary with sorrow; strengthen me according to your word".

Psalm 119:28 NIV

I watch the news and hear the names of our young heroes lost in the fighting. Even though I do not know these soldiers personally, I'm always overcome with tears of heavy grief. I sob with sorrow as I pray for their families and those who love them. I beg God to finish this war and allow our servicemen and women to come home safely. I plead for His protection over all of our courageous soldiers.

I'm racked with mourning for a child whom I never knew, and yet know all too well.

Praying daily for our soldiers is essential. Our soldiers need all our prayers. They need prayer for their physical safety. They need to be courageous. They need wisdom. They need to be of sound mind. They must remain strong. They have to remain committed and true to their cause. They need to know that their countrymen support and believe in them. They need to be released from daily worry about their families back home. They need to know that they are cherished.

Most of all, they need to know that God loves them! They need God's many blessings each and every day. Our military leaders, all the way up to the President, need our fervent prayers, as well. Please, pray daily for all of these things! May the peace and comfort of God be with all of us.

More Answered Prayer

"Then you will call and the Lord will answer; You will cry for help, and he will say: Here am I".

Isaiah 58:9 NIV

Isn't it nice when God sometimes answers our prayers almost instantly? I had just wished I could hear from my soldier, and there it was: handwriting I instantly recognized on a letter in my mailbox! Another time that same yearning was answered by a phone call out of the blue! Quickly answered prayer causes us to bless God's name and renews our faith in a very tangible way.

In other areas, however, God's answer to our

prayer is not clearly seen right away, if ever. These are the times when we must recall all those quickly answered prayers and reaffirm our belief that our Lord God is truly all-loving, all-knowing, and all-powerful.

As days of war drag into months and years; and the news gets worse instead of better, we must not forget why our soldiers are away. Always bear in mind the importance of what they are doing. Do not allow the confidence you have in our most gracious God to waiver. Persevere in your belief that His protection is covering your soldier, as well as mine. Continue to trust in God, who is shielding us all.

Our faith develops slowly in times like this, but as it grows, it becomes a clear, comforting, deeply rooted assurance that will carry us through anything that we face.

Without this dependence upon our Heavenly Father, we cannot muster the strength we will need for our day, but, thankfully, we can depend on the certainty that ours is a faith for today, a faith for all days.

Get Up!

"But you, O LORD, be not far off; O my Strength, come quickly to help me".

Psalm 22:19 NIV

How do we get through another day missing our soldier? Sometimes I just want to stay in bed under my covers! I know this does no good, though; I realize there are still chores to do, errands to run, bills to pay, and people to see. It is the simple daily routines that actually help the days to pass.

Whatever I am going through pales in comparison to what my soldier faces daily. I ponder on that for a moment and begin to chuckle. My soldier would kick me right out from under those covers!

Of course, when I consider the sufferings of my Savior Jesus Christ, I am put to shame. No pity-party for me today! Suddenly, I realize that I have miraculously gained the strength to get up and move. God gives us a beautiful new day; let us rejoice and be glad!

So, throw back those covers and get moving! Most likely, your soldier has been up and working hard for hours already! How dare you loll about, whining!

Get up, sing a song in the shower, have that first cup of coffee, and go have a wonderful day!

Lord, on those days when I just want to bury my head and sleep the day away, speak words of encouragement to me. Urge my heart to leap with joy, command my feet to dance, and guide my hands to serve. Remind me of the long hours my soldier endures, and bring me to my knees.

The Military Wife's Prayer

'Tis the still of the night, yet I am awake-
My hand stretches forth in search of my mate.
It's a habit that's grown,
This stroke of his hair,
Reassurance for me
Just to know he's still there…

But tonight he is not - his pillow is cold;
He's a soldier away, dedicated and bold.
Serving God and our country in a land far away
He can't come home yet, at war he must stay.

As I toss and roll over, I whisper a prayer

For the Lord to protect him-
Keep him safe over there.

In the palm of God's hand
And out of harm's way,
Grant him wisdom and peace,
Joy and strength for his day.

Joy Comes

A dear, elderly friend once was talking about her life. "Christ is my energy, my joy, my peace," she said. Her testimony touched my heart with its simple truth.

At moments when my own energy, joy and peace are at ebb low, all I have to do is remind myself that Christ is everything I need. When I do not have enough strength on my own, I can always ask to use *His*! My Lord has plenty of everything I need and is more than willing to share it all with me!

Whenever I pray for strength, or joy, or whatever; I also ask the Lord to give the same to my soldier. I imagine that whatever I need, my soldier probably needs at least as much!

Are you lacking faith today? Ask God to give you His. Strength? He has no weakness! Peace? Christ is peace! Are you feeling sad? Jesus delights in your joy, for your joy comes from Him! He loves to shower us with unlimited blessings!

Ask the Lord for whatever you need at this very moment. Now, be prepared to receive much more than you expected!

> *"The Lord is my strength and my shield; my heart trusts in him, and I am helped. My heart leaps for joy and I will give thanks to him in song"*
>
> Psalm 28:7 NIV

Extended Tour

"So we say with confidence, 'The Lord is my helper; I will not be afraid. What can man do to me?'".

Hebrews 13:6 NIV

The date is circled in red ink on your calendar. You've counted the days, planned the party, the day is nearing, and the excitement is mounting! You have been hanging on; waiting for the day your soldier will come home. You've gotten through family birthdays and other holidays with the thought that in only a few more weeks, you'd be celebrating them again with your loved one home. The light at the end of the long tunnel is growing brighter.

Then the dreaded words come: *tour extended.* The breath is knocked out of you. The emotions hit like a tidal wave; disbelief, denial, anguish, devastation, fury, exasperation, grief and heartbreak. Tears turn to heaving sobs, screams, stomping…

Now is not the time to be alone. Gather your supporting family and friends, or even just your closest friend to come stand beside you as quickly as possible.

You cannot kick the dog, break things, or punch holes in your walls. Nor is this the time to slump on the sofa and eat ice cream out of the box for days on end!

Your family and friends will be able to help find creative ways to vent your feelings in a healthy manner. There are many ways to express your feelings and begin to heal. Life will continue, and you must find how to pull yourself together.

One illustration of this is the mother of four who went to a boxing gym, donned gloves and took her frustration out on a punching bag until she had physically exhausted herself. Another person went to a desolated field and screamed as loud as he wanted. Some go running, others go to the gym for a hard work out or to the pool to swim laps. Whatever you choose to do, it seems that something physical is the best first choice. Later, when your body is tired, you can begin to work on the mental therapeutic process as well.

The Lord knows what you're feeling. Your angry feelings may be directed at the war, the terrorists, the military, its leaders, our president, and even at God Himself. He understands. It is okay to voice your feelings; the Lord will listen to whatever you need to say!

As the initial wave of outrageous feelings begins to subside, you will realize that God has been standing right there beside you the whole time. If you have been depending on His strength all along, you will feel it beginning to lift you again now. You can feel God's tender arms gathering you in, and you will be renewed in your inner being.

Take to heart the words from the psalmist, *"The LORD is my rock, my fortress and my deliverer; my God is my rock, in whom I take refuge"* (Psalm 18:2 NIV).

We can, indeed, take refuge in the Lord God. He will lift us up and lend us strength, especially when we understand that we have none of our own.

Be easy on yourself. As each day passes you will feel stronger. Carry on with your normal daily routine. Continue to wrap yourself in friends, family, work, hobbies, and prayer. Sooner than you think, a song will return to your heart, and a smile will replace the tears on your face.

Before very long, you will once again be counting the days, the hours, and then the minutes. The moment will come when you can once again throw your arms around your returned soldier!

> *"The LORD is my strength and my shield; my heart trusts in him, and I am helped. My heart leaps for joy and I will give thanks to him in song"*
>
> Psalm 28:7 NIV

Struggling

Here is a partial list of the things I've done to over-come my human weaknesses on days when I am missing my soldier: sitting in his room, driving his car, looking through old photo albums, open-ing his closet to catch a wisp of his smell, listen to his favorite music. All of these things can bring temporary comfort, but it is only when I turn my thoughts heavenward that I gain true relief.

God in His wisdom knows exactly what I need and when I need it. If I remember to ask, and stop depending on my own way of doing things, my God always delivers.

I often wonder how someone who has a soldier

away gets through life without a personal relationship with Christ. It just boggles my mind! I know that I certainly could not do it. If you are struggling, I pray that you will turn to the Lord and offer Him the opportunity to meet your needs today.

He has never failed me. I hope, like me, you will then want to live the rest of your life in gratitude to God for all He has done, is doing, and will continue to do in your life, my life, and the lives of our soldiers.

> *"Oh, taste and see that the LORD is good; Blessed is the man who trusts in Him!"*
>
> Psalm 34:8 NIV

Smiles

Smiles often make my day. The smile from a stranger can brighten a bleary moment. A smile from an infant reminds me of the hopes and dreams I've carried in my heart for my children since they were babies. A friendly store clerk's smile renews my faith in the goodness of people.

When I receive a smile from a friend, I am instantly comforted. The lovely smile of an elderly person teaches me that even our senior years can be filled with joy. A child's smile delights the soul, for it radiates with the simplicity of life.

I want to live a life that makes my Lord smile. To accomplish this, I must simply be obedient to the Word of God and keep my eyes on Him. Whenever I see the beauty of God's creations, whether it is in the sky, in the land, wildlife, or in the faces of mankind, I smile, for these things remind me that we are all loved.

Today, with each smile I see, I think of my own soldier's smiling face, and I am blessed with renewed strength and great happiness.

"I love you, O LORD, my strength".
Psalm 18:1 NIV

Politically Speaking

I overheard two people arguing over the politics of the war in Iraq. As I thought about their words, I realized that, to me, it does not matter if someone thinks the war is illegal, or right, who started it, or whether we went in under false pretenses or not. It's all just a lot of needless squabble. All arguments are pointless.

We are *at war*. I don't really care how people feel about this war. We all hate war. We all wish we lived in utopia, *but we don't.* However, the simple truth is that we are in a war, and so, we must now finish the task laid before us.

For many of us, this means that our beloved

is risking his or her life every moment of every day. Our soldiers are what matters, not our politics. Our soldiers need our constant prayers, our full support, the best equipment available, and our deepest gratitude.

If someone cannot offer their prayers, gratitude, and support to our soldiers, if they won't sacrifice anything for our country, they might as well stay away from me. I would have to tell them how I feel. As politely and succinctly as I could manage, I'd say, "Don't talk to me about the politics of war, and please don't call yourself a proud American in my presence."

> *"Who is this King of glory? The LORD strong and mighty, the LORD mighty in battle".*
>
> Psalm 24:8 NIV

Serenity

Serenity seems totally unattainable sometimes. It flits within our grasp, and then dances just out of reach, or disappears altogether. One of my goals in life is to become a more serene person.

To me, serenity is a combination, or culmination, of all the fruit of the Spirit: love, joy, peace, patience, kindness, gentleness, faithfulness, self-control, and goodness. All of these unite together to define, in my mind, at least, the true meaning of serenity.

Some day, I hope to be able to reflect back upon my life, look at the lives my children, and grandchildren, and be at peace. Even better, though, would be to look at my life today, at this very instant, and be able to be at peace with what I see now.

Even amidst the turmoil of everyday life, by diligently protecting and constantly striving to perfect these nine traits, these precious gifts, it is possible to obtain that allusive, yet oh so cherished treasure called serenity.

> *"But the fruit of the Spirit is love, joy, peace, long-suffering, kindness, goodness, faithfulness, gentleness, self-control".*
>
> Galatians 5:22, 23 NIV

What If the Worst Happens?

The depth of fear we walk through when our soldier is in moment-by-moment peril is mind boggling. It seems we live our lives holding our breath. We sigh from relief to see a new e-mail, and think, how did the families of soldiers manage before computers?

But what will happen if we are thrust into the worst trial of our lives? What if that dreaded government car should pull up and stop at our house?

A mama should not lose her baby.

I admit; I have struggled with God over this subject. I've wrestled, even fought with Him. From my frail, human point of view, I firmly believe that no parent should have a child die, no matter the age. I know this is not how the Almighty Father works, but I confess that I've argued for years over this with Him.

I've pushed God in the chest, pitching a full-fledged temper tantrum, and yelled, "When a parent does the right things, raises a good kid who lives to serve You, why do they have to suffer the loss of the child they've raised for You?"

He answers quietly, *"My will, not thine,"* as He draws me closer. As I continue to fight and argue, He ever so gently pulls me to His chest, until I collapse in sorrow and tears, and He holds me close as I bury my head on Him and cry.

I've heard it said that the scent in the air just before a hard rainstorm is what God smells like. That may be true, for when you have received the horrid news, and are left exhausted and sobbing on God's chest, the full brunt of the storm is only just beginning to howl in your life. I suppose that only those who have already ridden out this storm can fully understand the profundity of our human weakness, and fullness of God's sustaining strength.

The only way I would survive that storm would be to clutch God and bury my head into His chest and hang on for dear life. If I push Him away, I would drown in the storm of my sorrow. I know this in my head, I feel it in my heart, and I pray that, should the worst ever happen, I will have enough faith to cling to this truth.

"It is better to go to a house of mourning than to go to a house of feasting, for death is the destiny of every man; the living should take this to heart... When times are good, be happy; but when times are bad, consider: God has made the one as well as the other".

Ecclesiastes 7: 2, 14 NIV

Lord, I pray that the day never comes when my faith is tested in this manner. However, should that government car pull up in front of my home, and I know that the worst has happened, I pray that I will remember the faith of others who have walked this path before me, and how I hoped as I wrote these words that I would always faithfully cling to You. If I should someday re-read these words through tears of grief, may my heart be strengthened and comforted by Your Holy presence.

Holidays

We all try to prepare for upcoming holidays: your soldier's birthday, your anniversary, Christmas. Every holiday can be difficult, if we allow it to be. Even while our soldier is away, though, it is possible to truly enjoy these special days. We can rejoice with family and friends. We can use the occasion to reflect the peace of God to those around us.

Sometimes we put on a happy face only for the sake of our children during holidays. Perhaps that is necessary at times. But it is always better to be real. Children can sense when we are faking happiness. A perceptive child may feel resentful toward the soldier who is away.

I have found that I don't have to fake it if I have prepared myself mentally, spiritually, and physically, ahead of time. Spend a little more time in Bible study and prayer during the week before a special day.

Picture the upcoming festivities in your mind, and you may actually begin to look forward to them. Try to think of little things that can easily be done to make the day even merrier, like making party favors, baking a special treat, or picking up a few new decorations.

If you don't feel that you can honestly throw yourself into the holiday preparations, try seeking the aid of a buddy who is willing to help do the chores that you'd procrastinate on, like housecleaning or party supply shopping. Then, use the time for the special luxury of adult conversation and fellowship!

It is also important that we endeavor to have some "me time" beforehand. Try squeezing in an extra bit of exercise, a ten-minute walk, a few laps in the pool. Pay special attention to your diet, attempt to eat well, choose healthy foods. Try to catch some extra rest for a few days ahead of party time. Make an appointment to get your hair or nails done on the morning of the big day.

I have learned that I can handle stress better when I've taken just a little extra time to care for myself.

When the holiday arrives, allow yourself a special reward early in the day, so you don't have to feel rushed or hassled. For me, that means taking an extra, extra long, hot shower.

For you, it might be indulging in your favorite breakfast treat, taking a walk in the woods, keeping to that hair appointment you scheduled, or just lounging in bed for an extra twenty minutes!

This is also a good time to meditate on your favorite Bible passage, converse with the Lord, and ask for His special blessings to be upon you and your soldier throughout the day. We know how difficult the holidays can be for us, but we also realize that our soldiers may need an extra dose of God's grace and strength to make it through the day, as well.

If you've made all possible preparations, you're ready to enjoy the day, and you won't even have to fake a happy smile, because your joy will be genuine!

> *"There, in the presence of the LORD your God, you and your families shall eat and shall rejoice in everything you have put your hand to, because the LORD your God has blessed you".*
>
> Deuteronomy 12:7 NIV

Christmas in Baghdad

Far from home, no twinkling lights
No holiday rushing 'round-
It might be Christmastime back home,
But here can't be found.

There's dust and rubble in place of snow
No carolers' songs fill the street.
No Salvation Army donation bells-
Just a child who begs for a treat.

I give him a candy and tussle his hair,
How I wish I could see my boy!
"Merry Christmas," I say,

Though I wish I could give
A bike, or a Christmas toy.

He smiles bright and in English says,
"Thank You!" as he scampers away-
I give him a wave and continue patrol;
There's no break on Christmas Day.

I remember the Christmas pageant last year-
This year my daughter is singing.
But I'm doing my job and doing it proud
And the bells of freedom are ringing.

I love my family and I love my God
And I love my country true.
I'll celebrate Christmas in my heart
While I fight for the Red, White, and Blue.

A 'Mother Hen' Day

Today I've had my first 'Mother Hen' day. It started very early, before daybreak, when my radio softly relayed the news into my ear that another very serious terror threat had been thwarted. More reports of a possibly eminent nuclear attack are also swirling in the news. As the frightening reports continued throughout the day, my nerves slowly began to unravel.

I have a beloved son and son-in-law, as well as many other soldiers personally known to me facing deadly dangers of all kinds, and a daughter and granddaughter living across the ocean. I can't protect any of them.

Lord, I just want to pull 'all my chicks' home, tuck them safely under my wing, and hide for awhile! My 'boy' is unable to communicate with us, my sweet baby granddaughter is growing up in a strange and dangerous country, the whole world is in peril and all I want to do is bring all my babies home and hug them.

I pray. I read my emails, try to write a little, watch a mindless game show on T.V., vacuum every inch of my living room, struggle and ultimately fail to stay within the boundaries of my diet, (oh, excuse me: 'lifestyle change,') and meditate on my favorite Scripture verses. I thankfully have errands to run that will take me several hours this afternoon.

I know that this day will pass. My fears may abate slightly and my feelings of dread and foreboding will hopefully pass with the day. My God is still in control. It is okay that I am not in control. It is my choice to make today: will I trust God? Yes, I choose to trust Him.

A sigh of relief comes with that choice. A peace that is not of my own doing. A calmness in my soul that can only be called "supernatural." A sense of well-being that will carry me through another tough day.

I'm sure more 'Mother Hen' days lie ahead. No doubt that from time to time my faith will waver pitifully. Thankfully, I know that my Lord is not so much a 'Mother Hen,' but rather like a 'Father Eagle' and His wings are big enough to keep my whole flock safely protected. All I have to do is make the choice to trust Him, and I will once again receive all the strength I need.

> *"I carried you on eagles' wings and brought you to myself".*
>
> Exodus 1:4 NIV

Saying Goodbye

Saying good-bye is one thing we military families seem to do quite a bit of. If you're not saying farewell to your soldier, then you've said it to your parents, your friends, co-workers, church families, and many others as you have moved from one installation to another.

It is never easy and you never get used to it. Thankfully, the world of computers has made staying in touch easier on all of us. Some of us are allowed to IM, or Instant Message, our soldier, even from the battleground countries; others can at least email them. We can share news and updates with relative ease to a large group of our family and friends.

My family has built a website for our entire clan from all over the world. We use it to keep each other informed of family news. We plan future reunions through this site. We have a tribute page dedicated to our family's heroes who are serving our nation in many various ways. We can see all of our new babies in adorable photographs, and even though we live far apart, it has allowed us to get to know our more distant relatives, as well. I encourage you to build a family website of your own; it certainly is a wonderful thing!

My prayer as I say good-bye to you, dear reader, is that you have received encouragement and inspiration from these pages, and that your faith has been strengthened along the way.

Whenever I must say good-bye to a friend, I love to use this beautiful blessing from the apostle Paul:

"May the God of hope fill you with all joy and peace as you trust in him, so that you may overflow with hope by the power of the Holy Spirit".
                                    Romans 15:13 NIV

Made in the USA
San Bernardino, CA
11 December 2016